First World War
and Army of Occupation
War Diary
France, Belgium and Germany

23 DIVISION
Divisional Troops
Royal Army Veterinary Corps
35 Mobile Veterinary Section
27 August 1915 - 31 October 1917

WO95/2180/3

The Naval & Military Press Ltd
www.nmarchive.com
Published in association with The National Archives

Published by

The Naval & Military Press Ltd

Unit 10 Ridgewood Industrial Park,

Uckfield, East Sussex,

TN22 5QE England

Tel: +44 (0) 1825 749494

www.naval-military-press.com

www.nmarchive.com

This diary has been reprinted in facsimile from the original. Any imperfections are inevitably reproduced and the quality may fall short of modern type and cartographic standards.

© **Crown Copyright**
Images reproduced by permission of The National Archives, London, England, 2015.

Contents

Document type	Place/Title	Date From	Date To
Heading	WO95/2180/3 23 Division-Divisional Troops 35 Mobile Vetinary Section 1915 Aug-1917 Oct		
Heading	23rd Division 35th Mobile Vety Section Aug 1915-1917 Oct To Italy		
Heading	35 M Vet Sec Vol 6 23		
Heading	23rd Division 35th Mobile Vet. Sect. Vol I Aug Sep & Oct 15 Mar 19		
War Diary	Bordon	27/08/1915	27/08/1915
War Diary	Harve	28/08/1915	28/08/1915
War Diary	Tilque	29/08/1915	06/09/1915
War Diary	Merris	07/09/1915	15/09/1915
War Diary	Croix du Bac	16/09/1915	22/09/1915
War Diary	Hallebeau	25/09/1915	31/10/1915
Heading	23rd Div 35th Mobile Vet. Sect. Vol. 2& 3 Nov. Dec.		
War Diary	Hallebeau	01/11/1915	31/12/1915
Heading	35th Mob Vet. Sect. Vol 4		
War Diary	Hallebeau	01/01/1916	31/01/1916
War Diary	Croix Du Bac	01/02/1916	17/02/1916
War Diary	Steenbecque	18/02/1916	29/02/1916
War Diary	Bruay	01/03/1916	07/03/1916
War Diary	Caucourt	08/03/1916	15/03/1916
War Diary	Bruay	16/03/1916	21/03/1916
War Diary	Barlin	22/03/1916	18/04/1916
War Diary	Bruay	19/04/1916	30/04/1916
Miscellaneous	H.D.V.S. 23rd Division	20/08/1916	20/08/1916
War Diary	Bruay	01/05/1916	12/05/1916
War Diary	Barlin	13/05/1916	14/06/1916
War Diary	Bruay	15/06/1916	15/06/1916
War Diary	Bomy	16/06/1916	25/06/1916
War Diary	Vaux	26/06/1916	30/06/1916
War Diary	St Gratien	01/07/1916	05/07/1916
War Diary	Ribemont	06/07/1916	25/07/1916
War Diary	Ribemont	24/06/1916	14/08/1916
War Diary	Frechencourt	16/08/1916	16/08/1916
War Diary	Suerriou	17/08/1916	17/08/1916
War Diary	Godwaerswelde	18/07/1916	18/07/1916
War Diary	Pont Nieppe	19/08/1916	31/08/1916
War Diary	Nieppe	01/09/1916	06/09/1916
War Diary	Hazebrouck	07/09/1916	07/09/1916
War Diary	Nieppe	08/09/1916	11/09/1916
War Diary	Allonville	12/09/1916	13/09/1916
War Diary	St Gratien	14/09/1916	20/09/1916
War Diary	Albert	21/09/1916	09/10/1916
War Diary	St Gratien	11/10/1916	29/11/1916
Heading	War Diary from O.C. Mobile Veterinary Section November 1916		
War Diary	St Gratien	01/12/1916	05/12/1916
War Diary	Villas Bocage	07/12/1916	07/12/1916
War Diary	Barly	08/12/1916	08/12/1916
War Diary	Monchel	10/12/1916	10/12/1916

War Diary	Troisvoux	12/12/1916	12/12/1916
War Diary	Ligny Les Aire	13/12/1916	13/12/1916
War Diary	Thiennes	14/12/1916	14/12/1916
War Diary	Ryveld	16/12/1916	16/12/1916
War Diary	Steenwoorde	18/12/1916	27/12/1916
War Diary	Poperinghe	28/12/1916	31/12/1916
Heading	War Diary January 1917 O.C. 35 Mobile Veterinary Section Vol 15		
War Diary	Poperinghe	01/01/1917	28/01/1917
Heading	War Diary February 1917 O C 35 Mobile Veterinary Section		
War Diary	Poperinghe	01/02/1917	01/03/1917
War Diary	Herzeele	02/03/1917	02/03/1917
War Diary	Zeggars Cappel	03/03/1917	03/03/1917
War Diary	Houlle	04/03/1917	20/03/1917
War Diary	Lederzeele	21/03/1917	21/03/1917
War Diary	Herzeele	23/03/1917	10/04/1917
War Diary	Poperinghe	12/04/1917	30/04/1917
War Diary	Poperinghe	01/06/1917	02/06/1917
War Diary	Ryveld	04/06/1917	12/06/1917
War Diary	Renninghelst	14/06/1917	30/06/1917
War Diary	Renninghelst	01/06/1917	13/06/1917
War Diary	Berthen	15/06/1917	04/07/1917
War Diary	Reninghelst.	04/07/1917	23/07/1917
War Diary	Berthen	24/07/1917	03/08/1917
War Diary	Arques	05/08/1917	05/08/1917
War Diary	Nr Harlette	06/08/1917	06/08/1917
War Diary	Eperleques	09/08/1917	20/08/1917
War Diary	Noorpeene	23/08/1917	23/08/1917
War Diary	Reninghelst	24/08/1917	31/08/1917
War Diary	Lederzeele	05/09/1917	12/09/1917
War Diary	La Clytte	14/09/1917	22/09/1917
War Diary	Moved to West Noutre	25/09/1917	25/09/1917
War Diary	West Noutre	26/09/1917	27/09/1917
War Diary	Moved To La Blytte	28/09/1917	28/09/1917
War Diary	La Blytte	29/09/1917	30/09/1917
War Diary	Moved To Berthen	01/10/1917	02/10/1917
War Diary	Berthen	03/10/1917	05/10/1917
War Diary	La Blytte	01/10/1917	01/10/1917
War Diary	To Berthen	02/10/1917	06/10/1917
War Diary	To La Clytte	07/10/1917	17/10/1917
War Diary	La Clytte	18/10/1917	22/10/1917
War Diary	Quercamps	23/10/1917	26/10/1917
War Diary	Wizernes	27/10/1917	31/10/1917

WO 95 2180/3

23 Division - Divisional Troops

35 MOBILE VETINARY SECTION

1915 AUG - 1917 OCT

23RD DIVISION

35TH MOBILE VETY SECTION

AUG 1915-~~MAR 1919~~
1917 OCT

To ITALY

35 M Versie
vol 5 6
23

121/7595

23rd Kareum

35th Mobile Vet. Sech.
Vol I
Aug, Sept & Oct 15

Nov '19

WAR DIARY
or
INTELLIGENCE SUMMARY.

(Erase heading not required.)

Army Form C. 2118.

Place	Date	Hour	Summary of Events and Information	Remarks and references to Appendices
Boulan	27.8	12 AM	Left Boulan with two lorries & waggon in about 4. P.M. Embarked on the train & alabim for Rouen. The train arriving there about 2. A.M. Disembarking	
Rouen	28.8		arrives Rouen about 2. A.M. Disembarked 07 A.M. Disembarking wagons.	
Rouen	29.8		Arrived Pt 6 mm 3. P.M. and unworked at I legun Billi, camping.	
"	30.8		Nothing of change. Some lorries away to unload munitions	
"	31.8		Received two lorries from Supply Corps R.E. One lorry and one motor-bike from Rouen.	
"	1.9		Received one waggon from 190 Coy A.S.C. & lorry and truck	
"	2.9		Received one waggon from 190 Coy A.S.C supplying from Guellen	
"	3.9		Changes some lorries away to unload munitions	
"	4.9		Everything following.	
"	5.9		Received 16 lorries went to Rouen to pick up from waggon (Ketu) Conveying 16 animals to Base	

Army Form C. 2118

WAR DIARY
or
INTELLIGENCE SUMMARY.
(Erase heading not required.)

Instructions regarding War Diaries and Intelligence Summaries are contained in F. S. Regs., Part II. and the Staff Manual respectively. Title pages will be prepared in manuscript.

Place	Date	Hour	Summary of Events and Information	Remarks and references to Appendices
Jegun	6-9		Received 7 sick animals 3 from 104 Pack & 1-103 Pack 1-105 Pack & 1-DAC. 1-70 F.A. Grenadiers, 12 animals to Mouned troops. Horses is sepoys in lines afternoon	
huri	7-9		Marched to Mourez about 8 A.m. arrived 1 P.M. Arranged billets for men & horses	
"	8-9		Made out in search of unli supply for more from 2 places but without success for want of horse	
"	9-9		Received 10 sick animals, weak supplies from myn given	
"	10-9		Sent to animal to Mourved's hospital. Calcutta 3 sick animals	
"	11-9		Only 10 horses chiefly Expe goer & Rick & sent 3 animals to hospital hospital	
"	12-9		Only 1 horse from 19 OBg A.S.C. suffering from huy apa. Grenadiers 28 animals to hospital	

WAR DIARY
INTELLIGENCE SUMMARY

Army Form C. 2118.

Place	Date	Hour	Summary of Events and Information	Remarks and references to Appendices
Mervis	13-9		Admitted 16 wounded	
"	14-9		Admitted 10 wounded & evacuated 15	
"	15-9		Lent Surg. & 6 Bearers to No. 3 Fd Amb, receiving station. Admitted 10 wounded	
Croix du Bac	16-9		Marched from Mervis to Croix du Bac & staff arrived on evacuation of 2 nuns & admitted 10 wounded & fired three tents	
"	17-9		Admitted 10 wounded	
"	18-9		Admitted 7 wounded and evacuated to Army Fd Ambce receiving barge	
"	19-9		Admitted 6 wounded & sent 11 nuns to Fd Ambce receiving	
"	20-9		Admitted 7 wounded & evacuated 11 wounded to Fd Ambce receiving	
"	21-9		Admitted 2 wounded	

WAR DIARY
or
INTELLIGENCE SUMMARY

Army Form C. 2118

Place	Date	Hour	Summary of Events and Information	Remarks and references to Appendices
Croix de Bac	22.9		Admitted 16 animals and sent 15 animals to the Vet. Hospital	
"	23.9		Admitted 2.0 animals and convalesced 6.	
"	24.9		Admitted 2 animals and there one wire A.D.V.S. accompanied visited 2 Fd Amm. Coys for observation during an exercise in shelling. Observed during an exercise in horsemanship.	
Sailleval	25.9		Proceeded to Sailleval accompanied by our vehicles. An I.N.C.O & 2 men proceeded to Provision Fruits Arrived at Sailleval, water from pumps will supplement water from clinical examined	
"	26.9		Admitted 5 horses & evacuated 2 animals. Visited the Brais and traced out causes of various observed clinical symptoms from Shrapnel wounds belonging to 10th Bde.	

WAR DIARY
or
INTELLIGENCE SUMMARY

Army Form C. 2118

Place	Date	Hour	Summary of Events and Information	Remarks and references to Appendices
Hellebus	27-9		Nuclei advances collecting & clearing stations from all corned. Shelter 12 horses, mules supplying from Rear on evacuated to convert to Base Vet. Hosps.	
"	28-9		Nuclei advanced dressing stations in operation with A.D.S. from all corned. Admitted 12 horses and mules — evacuated away 16 horses & mules — Res. complete.	
"	29-9		Nuclei advanced dressing station all coned. Admitted to date on recd: 14 horses & mules. Res. complete	
"	30-9		Nuclei advancing division to advance. & arm	
"	1-10		2 nuclei advancing to divisions & supplying to advance. Admitted 11 horses and mules	

Army Form C. 2118

WAR DIARY
or
INTELLIGENCE SUMMARY.
(Erase heading not required.)

Instructions regarding War Diaries and Intelligence Summaries are contained in F. S. Regs., Part II. and the Staff Manual respectively. Title pages will be prepared in manuscript.

Place	Date	Hour	Summary of Events and Information	Remarks and references to Appendices
Helleben	2-10		Calcutta 6 onward to wounded 10 Li Born	
"	3-10		Calcutta 6 wounded & conv: 6 to Bom vols enquire hove gross difficulty in getting some ambulance.	
"	4-10		Calcutta 10 Bom	
"	5-10		Calcutta 10 onward to conv: conv convalescents 16 Li Bom vols Enquire	
"	6-10		Calcutta 2 sent on wounded 11	
"	7-10		Calcutta 2 Bom	
"	8-10		Calcutta 5 onward & Conv: 7 Li Bom vols Enqu	
"	9-10		Calcutta 4 wounded	
"	10-10		Calcutta 15 onward & convalescents 16.	
"	11-10		Calcutta 7 onward & convalescents 11	
"	12-10		Calcutta 15 onward on convalescents 8	

Army Form C. 2118

WAR DIARY
or
INTELLIGENCE SUMMARY.
(Erase heading not required.)

Instructions regarding War Diaries and Intelligence Summaries are contained in F. S. Regs., Part II. and the Staff Manual respectively. Title pages will be prepared in manuscript.

Place	Date	Hour	Summary of Events and Information	Remarks and references to Appendices
Hellebera	13-10		[shorthand]	
"	14-10		[shorthand]	
"	15-10		[shorthand]	
"	16-10		[shorthand]	
"	17-10		[shorthand]	
"	18-10		[shorthand]	
"	19-10		[shorthand]	
"	20-10		[shorthand]	
"	21-10		[shorthand]	
"	22-10		[shorthand]	
"	23-10		[shorthand]	
"	25-10		[shorthand]	
"	26-10		[shorthand]	

Army Form C. 2118.

WAR DIARY
or
INTELLIGENCE SUMMARY.
(Erase heading not required.)

Place	Date	Hour	Summary of Events and Information	Remarks and references to Appendices
Gallipoli	27-10		Admitted 1 man	
"	28-10		Admitted 0 men	
"	29-10		Admitted 0 men & evacuated 2 men C. N.Y.S. Only frost-strippers in present	
"	30-10		Admitted 2 men	
"	31-10		Admitted 1 man & sent to C N.Y.S. do.	

35th Mobile Vet: Sec:
Vol: 243
Nov. Dec

23rd Div

Army Form C. 2118.

WAR DIARY
or
INTELLIGENCE SUMMARY.
(Erase heading not required.)

Instructions regarding War Diaries and Intelligence Summaries are contained in F. S. Regs., Part II. and the Staff Manual respectively. Title pages will be prepared in manuscript.

Place	Date	Hour	Summary of Events and Information	Remarks and references to Appendices
Mullean	1-11-15	-	Received Dy. Ord. admitting one horse from 104 Bde A.C. & Lynard Corps.	
	2-11-15		Admitted 2 horses from 102 Bde A C & 102 Bde R A & invalids 3 horses to Base Vet: Hospital. Inspected R.E. & men kits also water & cook-rooms.	
	3-11-15		Admitted 6 horses (sick) & 5 horses other than Vet: Rems. Sent 5 horses to D.D.R.	
	4-11-15		Admitted 7 sick horses & 6 horses for other than Vet: Rems. Invalided 11 animals — 5 horses & 6 mules.	
	5-11-15		Admitted 4 horses. Inspected men in marching order.	
	6-11-15		Admitted 1 Officer & invalided 6 horses & 1 Base Vet: Hosp. Rain heavily.	
	7-11-15			
	8-11-15		Admitted 2 horses – 1 Enfield & 1 Imp'd Corps.	
	9-11-15		Admitted 1 horse from 140 Comp. A.S.C. Gave lecture to men on Sanitary work.	

Army Form C. 2118.

WAR DIARY
or
INTELLIGENCE SUMMARY.
(Erase heading not required.)

Instructions regarding War Diaries and Intelligence Summaries are contained in F.S. Regs., Part II. and the Staff Manual respectively. Title pages will be prepared in manuscript.

Place	Date	Hour	Summary of Events and Information	Remarks and references to Appendices
Gallebe	10-11-15		Admitted to field Amee & Evacuated & Base li Base Vets Infirie. New private difficulty in obtaining Ambulance.	
	11-11-15		Admitted 5 horses needing shoeing / chaffed womens sick. 1 horse li Base Vets Infirie.	
	12-11-15		Admitted 3 anis. Inspected men at mounted drill.	
	13-11-15		Admitted 2 anis.	
	14-11-15		Sent 5 horses out / mule li Base Vets Hospital.	
	15-11-15		Admitted 11 horses one to other than Vets anum.	
	16-11-15		Admitted 1 horse from Cable section & sent 14 horses li Base Vets Hospital.	
	17-11-15		Admitted 16 horses & 1 mule & sent li Base Vets Hospital 13 animals.	
	18-11-15		Sent 3 mules away & horse li Base li Base Hospital & admitted 5 horses & 2 mules.	

WAR DIARY
or
INTELLIGENCE SUMMARY.
(Erase heading not required.)

Army Form C. 2118.

Place	Date	Hour	Summary of Events and Information	Remarks and references to Appendices
Gallipoli	19-11-15		Admitted 13 wounded including one Shrapnel wound. Evacuated 2 mules & 51 men to Base Vets Hosp	
	20-11-15		Admitted 10 horses and 1 mule. Evacuated to 15 horses & 1 mule to Base Vets Hospital. How li chully 1 store suffering from weakness (Pneumonia) one of the horse admitted suffering from shrapnel wound.	
	21-11-15		Admitted 4 horses & 1 mule other Vets cases. Sub-li Bn Vets Hospital signed over by li smith to different Officer Lt Capn Stemmen ambulance.	
	22-11-15		Admitted 17 animals all horses.	
	23-11-15		Admitted 25 animals mules suffering from debility. Sub li Bn Vets Hospital 3 S.R. Infantry animals & 1 horse li S.R. Infantry L.C.V.S. Infirm animals Details, Debility /Shells own in arms	

WAR DIARY
or
INTELLIGENCE SUMMARY

(Erase heading not required.)

Army Form C. 2118.

Place	Date	Hour	Summary of Events and Information	Remarks and references to Appendices
Abbé Guillaume	24-11-15		Admitted 3 & evacuated nine suffering from shell shock one during enemy's aeroplane raid. Prepared during the evening to Rue des Tranchées. During the night men were employed making a tunnel which leads to Rue des Tranchées.	
	25-11-15		Admitted 6 wounded. Evacuated suffering men. Obtaining ambulance.	
	26-11-15		Admitted 5 men & 2 mules wounded & evacuated to Rue des Tranchées. Four mules & 2 men were suffering from gases, two children were wounded & 2 mules which were evacuated.	
	27-11-15		Admitted 6 nurses & 2 mules suffering from shrapnel wounds (women).	
	28-11-15		Admitted 3 nurses & 2 mules evacuated 2 nurses to F.A. and 1 nurse & four mules to Rue des Tranchées	

Army Form C. 2118.

WAR DIARY
or
INTELLIGENCE SUMMARY.
(Erase heading not required.)

Instructions regarding War Diaries and Intelligence Summaries are contained in F. S. Regs., Part II. and the Staff Manual respectively. Title pages will be prepared in manuscript.

Place	Date	Hour	Summary of Events and Information	Remarks and references to Appendices
Fulleham	29-11-15		Calmettes 2.6 onward – Snipers 2.3 – Trench 3 all else above were chiefly line of Rebels	
	30-11-15		Calmettes 15 Rounds – Rebels	
	1-19-15		Calmettes 11 Rounds and 2 mile	
	1-12-15		Rounds to Snipers & 3 miles Ridges & order of A.V.S. 3 Rifles – F	
	2-12-15		Calmettes 5.3 onward 8.9 snipers & 15 miles how is distance and snipers from 10.6 Bde suffering from an Enfilade (Enghien) fire from N.S. Enfield 4.5 Snipers are all close over own trench Snipers are falling 2 & snipers of Rebels	
	3-12-15		Calmettes 26 Snipers and 1 mile – Rebels Snipers in Rue Vas (suffering 2 & snipers of 3 mile and in direction Snipers 10.3 Rifle &c known to bearer	

WAR DIARY
or
INTELLIGENCE SUMMARY.
(Erase heading not required.)

Army Form C. 2118.

Place	Date	Hour	Summary of Events and Information	Remarks and references to Appendices
Gallipoli	4-12-15		Casualties 3 horses	
"	5-12-15		Casualties 3 horses wounded 6 horses & 1 mule	
			ponies died	
"	6-12-15		Casualties 2 horses from debility & 1st Aid	
"	7-12-15		Casualties 7 horses & 2 mules	
"	8-12-15		Casualties 5 horses & 1 cob died. Received Vet. hospital	
			6 horses & 2 mules	
"	9-12-15		Casualties 1 horse & evacuated 6 horses.	
"	10-12-15		Casualties 2 horses	
"	11-12-15		Casualties 10 horses & 1 mule died. 7 horses	
			to Base Vet. Hospital	
"	12-12-15		Casualties 10 horses & 6 mules died. Base Vet. Hospital	
			6 mules	

WAR DIARY
or
INTELLIGENCE SUMMARY

Army Form C. 2118.

Place	Date	Hour	Summary of Events and Information	Remarks and references to Appendices
Gallipoli	13-12-15		Casualties 5 officers & 5 men wounded, 7 men missing	
"	14-12-15		Casualties 16 men & 1 Lieut: 5 officers & 2 men in Braw Vols infantile	
"	15-12-15		Casualties 11 men & 5 men including 1 case of Enteric wounded – Evacuated 15 Enteric	
"	16-12-15		Casualties & men	
"	17-12-15		Casualties 10 men & Lieut 14 men & 4 men in Braw Vols infantile, 2nd Lieut C. clarifying one man from 102 Btln. Suffering from Paralysis	
"	18-12-15		Casualties 10 officers & Lieut. 6 men L. Brown Vols infantile	
"	19-12-15		Casualties 2, 3 men & 2 men from F.A.C. & wounded 5 men & 19 men Arm & shoulder, one officer of Imperial Camp – wounded & evacuated	

WAR DIARY
or
INTELLIGENCE SUMMARY

Army Form C. 2118.

Place	Date	Hour	Summary of Events and Information	Remarks and references to Appendices
Mulgheen	20-12-15		Calcutta 71 animals from A.A.C. 17 horses & 56 mule. All the above were sick & debility. Casualties 7, 9 animals. 2 horses & 51 mule.	
"	21-12-15		Calcutta 11 horses & mule to horse to the Horse Vets hospital all of which were suffering from debility.	
"	22-12-15		Calcutta 9 horse & 1 mule & evacuated to hospital	
"	23-12-15		Calcutta 14 mule & 13 horses & mule, di the Base Vets hospital. 32 animals	
"	24-12-15		Calcutta 6 horses & 1 mule	
"	25-12-15		Calcutta 1 horse from A.A.R.7 A mules & 2 mule & sent to the	
"	26-12-15		Calcutta 7 horses & mule. B un Vets hospital 21 horse & 2 mule. How to chatting 1 horse from 140 Coy ASC away to cyprus Spain.	

WAR DIARY or INTELLIGENCE SUMMARY

Army Form C. 2118.

Place	Date	Hour	Summary of Events and Information	Remarks and references to Appendices
Hallebrun	27-12-15		Admitted 11 sick & invalids 8 horses & mules	
"	28-12-15		Admitted 6 sick & invalids including 2 shrapnel wounds & invalids 6 horses	
"	29-12-15		Admitted 29 sick of which 3 horses over for other Vet Rsn. & Invalids 23 horses. Evacuated 12 horses & 3 mules to Base Vet Hospital	
"	30-12-15			
"	31-12-15		Admitted 15 sick & invalids 20 animals went on temp. duty Capt Allemand A.V.C. to dept. afri Station	

35th Instr: Vetr: Seer.

Vol: I

Army Form C. 2118.

WAR DIARY
or
INTELLIGENCE SUMMARY.
(Erase heading not required.)

31st Motor Amb. Section

Place	Date	Hour	Summary of Events and Information	Remarks and references to Appendices
Gallipoli	1-1-16	—	On leave Capt Allaun attached to duty as M.O. Ref. Section	
"	2-1-16		Admitted 13 horses sick and evacuated to Divn Mobile 2 horses & 13 mules to M.Ref. Section	
"	3-1-16		Admitted 7 animals. 6 horses & 1 mule	
"	4-1-16		Admitted 7 horses and sent 13 horses & 1 mule to Divn Vet. Hospital	
"	5-1-16		Admitted 3 horses. Divn Vet. Section & Ambulance	
"	6-1-16		Admitted 9 animals	
"	7-1-16		Admitted 8 animals. Sent 17 animals to Divn Vet Hospital	
"	8-1-16		Admitted 4 horses	
"	9-1-16		Admitted 6 animals & evacuated 15 animals over sea line from Cape Hellen	
"	10-1-16		Admitted 10 animals	
"	11-1-16		Admitted 7 animals on sent 14 horses & 1 mule to Divn Vet. Hospital	
"	12-1-16		Admitted 4 horses and 1 mule	

Army Form C. 2118.

WAR DIARY
or
INTELLIGENCE SUMMARY.
(Erase heading not required.)

31st Welsh Fd. [Ambulance]

Place	Date	Hour	Summary of Events and Information	Remarks and references to Appendices
Gallipoli	13-1-16		Admitted 28 animals and evacuated 26 horses & 1 mule to Base.	
"	14-1-16		Admitted 6 animals and evacuated 3 horses & ambulance shoe pencil (?) also put 3 horses down in enemy ambulance	
"	15-1-16		Admitted 14 horses & 2 mules Evacuated 13 horses & 1 mule	
"	16-1-16		Admitted 6 horses and other animals	
"	17-1-16		Admitted 5 horses and challenging 3 horses to ent. 12 horses and 3 mules to Base Fd - Hospital	
"	18-1-16		Admitted 11 horses and 1 mule	
"	19-1-16		Evacuated 7 horses and 1 mule	
"	20-1-16		Admitted 5 animals & sent to base to base to Base Vet. Hosp. horses 2 mules & horse ambulance	
"	21-1-16		Admitted 5 horses	
"	22-1-16		Admitted 5 animals	

Army Form C. 2118.

WAR DIARY
or
INTELLIGENCE SUMMARY.
(Erase heading not required.)

Instructions regarding War Diaries and Intelligence Summaries are contained in F. S. Regs., Part II. and the Staff Manual respectively. Title pages will be prepared in manuscript.

Place	Date	Hour	Summary of Events and Information	Remarks and references to Appendices
Hellburn	23-1-16		Admitted 4 animals & Public Stables	
"	24-1-16		Admitted 6 horses & Convalescin 14 horses to Base	
"	25-1-16		Admitted 11 horses & 2 mules & sent 16 horses d 1 mule to Base	
"	26-1-16		Admitted 11 horses & sent 7 horses to Base	
"	27-1-16		Admitted 5 horses & 1 mule & Convalescin 6 horses	
"	28-1-16		Admitted 8 horses & 1 mule & sent 10 horses & 3 mules to Base	
"	29-1-16		Admitted 6 horses & 2 mules. Wants to catch R.B.W.	
"	30-1-16		Admitted 4 horses & 3 mules & Convalescin 10 horses & 8 mules	
"	31-1-16		Admitted 2 horses	

2353 Wt. W3544/1454 700,000 5/15 D.D. & L. A.D.S.S./Forms/C. 2118.

Army Form C. 2118.

WAR DIARY
or
INTELLIGENCE SUMMARY.
(Erase heading not required.)

35 Mobile Veterinary Section
February 1916.

Instructions regarding War Diaries and Intelligence Summaries are contained in F.S. Regs., Part II. and the Staff Manual respectively. Title pages will be prepared in manuscript.

Place	Date	Hour	Summary of Events and Information	Remarks and references to Appendices
CROIX du BAC	Feb 1/16		Admitted 6 HORSES, 3 Mules. Evacuated to B.V.H. 8 Horses, 4 Mules.	
"	" 2		" 2 " Nil	
"	" 3		" 8 " , 2 Mules. Evacuated " 7 " 1 "	
"	" 4		" 4 " Nil	
"	" 5		" 5 " Evacuated " 11 "	
"	" 6		" 7 " Evacuated " 16 " 1 "	
"	" 7		" 2 " 4 Mules. Evacuated " 10 " 4 "	
"	" 8		" 3 " Nil	
"	" 9		" 6 " Evacuated " 5 "	
"	" 10		" 11 " Nil	
"	" 11		" 8 " 2 Mules. " 16 "	
"	" 12		" 8 " Nil Evacuated " 21 " 2 Mules	
"	" 13		" 6 " Nil	
"	" 14		" 4 " Evacuated " 13 "	
"	" 15		" 9 " Nil	
"	" 16		" 4 " Evacuated " 9 "	
"	" 17		Handed over 6 sick mules to 44 DVS. Transferred from CROIX du BAC post to billets at STEENBECQUE 1 Mule	
STEENBECQUE	" 18		Admitted 1 Horse	
"	" 19		" 1 "	
"	" 20		" 1 "	
"	" 21		" 4 "	
"	" 22		" 6 " 2 Mules	
"	" 23		" 4 "	
"	" 24		Evacuated to B.V.H. 11 Horses, 3 Mules.	
"	" 25		Admitted 1 Horse	
"	" 26		" 9 "	
"	" 27		" 5 " 1 Mule. Evacuated to B.V.H. 10 Horses	
"	" 28		" 7 " Section to headquarters ST VENANT 7 Lieut & 2 Mules. Left on tour with Madame Kokers de Farme STEENBECQUE 1915	
"	" 29		Mobilized to B.V.H. Section to Headquarters ST TSRAY. Brought one mule from such as ...	

R.C. Allinson
Capt. A.V.C.
O.C. 35 Mobile Veterinary Section

Army Form C. 2118.

WAR DIARY
or
INTELLIGENCE SUMMARY
(Erase heading not required.)

Instructions regarding War Diaries and Intelligence Summaries are contained in F. S. Regs., Part II. and the Staff Manual respectively. Title Pages will be prepared in manuscript.

Place	Date	Hour	Summary of Events and Information	Remarks and references to Appendices
Bruay	1.3.16		Look up fresh Billets	
"	2.3.16		Admitted (1) Horse	
"	3.3.16		Admitted (1) Horse & (1) Mule	
"	4.3.16		Drawing Hay fm Stables & Preparing Same	
"	6.3.16		Admitted (2) Horses Evacuated (7) Horses & (1) Mule to B.V. Hospl.	
"	8.3.16		Admitted (2) Horses & (1) Mule	
"	7.3.16		Admitted (2) Horses	
Caucourt	8.3.16		Marched to Caucourt. Evacuated (7) Horses & (1) Mule to B.V. Hospl.	
"	9.3.16		Cleaning up Stables & Lines	
"	10.3.16		Admitted (1) Horse	
"	11.3.16		Admitted (1) Horse & (1) Mule	
"	12.3.16		Admitted (2) Horses	
"	13.3.16		Admitted (1) Horse & (1) Mule. Destroyed same	
"	14.3.16		Admitted (6) Horses	
"	15.3.16		Admitted (8) Horses & (1) Mule Evacuated (1) Horse & (1) Mule to B.V.H.	
Bruay	16.3.16		Marched to Bruay. Handed over (3) Sick Horses to No 7 Div Mobile took over (1) Mule (2) Sick Horses from No 7 Div Mobile. Admitted (1) Horse & being (1) Horse fm Mattu keel no re admn	

R. Allison
Capt AVC

Army Form C. 2118.

WAR DIARY
or
INTELLIGENCE SUMMARY
(Erase heading not required.)

Instructions regarding War Diaries and Intelligence Summaries are contained in F.S. Regs., Part II. and the Staff Manual respectively. Title Pages will be prepared in manuscript.

Place	Date	Hour	Summary of Events and Information	Remarks and references to Appendices
Bray	17.3.16		Admitted (8) Sick Horses	
"	18.3.16		Admitted (6) Sick Horses & (1) Mule	
"	19.3.16		Admitted (9) Sick Horses Handed over (16) Sick Horses & 2nd Divl Mob. Evacuated (26) Horses & (1) Mule to B.V.H.	
"	20.3.16		Drawing Stay & repairing Cables	
"	21.3.16		Admitted (1) Sick Horse Handed over (1) Horse after Mobln Sect 16 & 7 Divl Mob.	
Barlin	22.3.16		Marched to Barlin Admitted (9) Sick Horse	
"	23.3.16		Admitted (3) Horses & (1) Mule Sick	
"	24.3.16		Admitted (4) Sick Horses & (1) Mule	
"	25.4.16		Admitted (16) Sick Horses & 1 Mule Evacuated Sick (22) Horses & 3 Mules to B.V.H.	
"	26.3.16		Admitted (4) Sick Horses	
"	27.3.16		Admitted (11) Horses & (2) Mules Sick Evacuated (13) Horses & (2) Mules to B.V.H.	
"	28.3.16		Admitted (10) Horses & (1) Mule	
"	29.3.16		Evacuated (11) Horses & (1) Mule to Base Vet Hospt.	
"	30.3.16		Admitted (9) Horses & (1) Mule	
"	31.3.16		Admitted (6) Horses & (1) Mule Evacuated (16) Horses & (2) Mules	

R. C. Allman
Capt A.V.C

35 Mobile Veterinary Section

35 M Vet Sect
Vol 6

WAR DIARY or INTELLIGENCE SUMMARY
(Erase heading not required.)

Army Form C. 2118.

Place	Date	Hour	Summary of Events and Information	Remarks and references to Appendices
Bar lins	1.4.16		Admitted (5) Sick Horses. Re issued (1) Horse to 98 Div Signals	
"	2.4.16		Admitted (3) Sick Horses & (1) Mule. Destroyed (1) Horse Injuries	
"	3.4.16		Admitted (3) Sick Horses & (1) Mule. Evacuated (6) Horses (2) Mules to 13 V. Hospl	
"	4.4.16		Admitted (7) Sick Horses & (1) Mule. Evacuated (7) Horses & (1) Mule to B.V. Hospl	
"	5.4.16		Admitted (1) Sick Horse & (1) Mule	
"	6.4.16		Admitted (4) Sick Horses. Evacuated (8) Horses & (1) Mule to B.V. Hospl.	
"	7.4.16		Admitted (10) Sick Horses	
"	8.4.16		Admitted (4) Sick Horses. Evacuated (14) Horses to Base Vet Hospital	
"	9.4.16		Admitted (10) Sick Horses	
"	10.4.16		Admitted (3) Sick Horses. Evacuated (14) Horses to Base Vet Hospital	
"	11.4.16		Admitted (4) Sick Horses & (3) Mules	
"	12.4.16		Admitted (5) Sick Horses	
"	13.4.16		Admitted (7) Sick Horses & (1) Mule. Evacuated (17) Horses & (4) Mule to 13 V. Hospl	
"	14.4.16		Admitted (5) Sick Horses	
"	15.4.16		Admitted (5) Sick Horses	
"	16.4.16		Admitted (16) Sick Horses & (2) Mules. Evacuated (19) Sick Horses & (1) Mule to B.V Hospl	
"	17.4.16		Admitted (4) Horses & (1) Mule. Evacuated (4) Horses sick to B.V. Hospl	
"	18.4.16		Admitted (6) Sick Horses & (1) Mule. Evacuated (10) Sick Horses & (2) Mules to B.V. Hospl	
Bruay	19.4.16		Admitted (2) Sick Horses Handed over (3) Sick Horses to 3.M.V.S. Evacuated (2) Horses sick to DDVS	
"	20.4.16		Admitted (1) Mule	
"	21.4.16		Admitted (1) Horse & (1) Mule	

A. T. Atkinson
OC 35 MVS

Army Form C. 2118.

WAR DIARY
or
INTELLIGENCE SUMMARY

(Erase heading not required.)

Instructions regarding War Diaries and Intelligence Summaries are contained in F. S. Regs., Part II. and the Staff Manual respectively. Title Pges will be prepared in manuscript.

Place	Date	Hour	Summary of Events and Information	Remarks and references to Appendices
Bruay	22.4.16		Repairing Horse Standings	
"	23.4.16		Admitted (2) Sick Horses	
"	24.4.16		Admitted (1) Sick Horses	
"	25.4.16		Admitted (3) Sick Horses & (1) Mule Evacuated (4) Sick Horses & (2) Sick to B.V. Hospital	
"	26.4.16		Admitted (6) Sick Horses	
"	27.4.16		Admitted (3) Sick Horses Evacuated (6) Sick Horses & (1) Mule to B.V. Hospital	
"	28.4.16		Admitted (3) Sick Horses	
"	29.4.16		Admitted (7) Sick Horses & (1) Mule Evacuated (11) Horses & (1) Mule to B.V. Hospital	
"	30.4.16		Admitted (3) Sick Horses & (1) Mule	

R.C. Allison
Capt. A.V.C.
O.C.
S.S.M.V.S.

B/30/11

H.Q.S. 23rd Division

Enclosed find War Diary for
May, June & July.
The reason I did not send it
through each month was -
the May Diary was returned
& I was informed that a G.R.O.
was issued relating to it, on looking
this up I thought it meant that the
Diary was no longer required to
be kept for a M.V.S.

20.8.16
R.P. Allinson
Capt. A.V.C.

A.A. & Q.M.G.

Herewith diary from the 35th M.V.S.
for the months of May, June & July
with above explanation for delay
by the O.C. of Section.

F.W. Ritchie
Major
A.D.V.S. 23rd Division

20.8.16

23 MAY / JUNE
Army Form C. 2118.

M.V. SECTION

Vol 7.8.9

R.Mure
Captains

WAR DIARY
or
INTELLIGENCE SUMMARY
(Erase heading not required.)

Place	Date	Hour	Summary of Events and Information	Remarks and references to Appendices
Bruay	1.5.16	—	Admitted (4) Horses (2) Mules 23 Div	
"	2		Admitted (3) Horses (1) Mule 23 Div Evacuated (10) Horses (4) Mules to Base Vety Hospital	
"	3		Admitted (5) Horses 23 Div	
"	4		Admitted (2) Horses (1) Mule 23 Div	
"	5		Admitted (4) Horses (1) Mule P. (3) 23 Div (2) 33 Siege Batt. Evacuated (2) Horses (2) Mules to Base Vet Hosp	
"	6		Admitted (3) Horses 23 Div Received (1) Horse	
"	7		Admitted (6) Horses (4) Mules 23 Div Evacuated (9) Horses (2) Mules to Base Vet Hosp Received (1) Mule	
"	8		Admitted (1) Horse 23 Div	
"	9		Admitted (13) Horses each (8) Coal Horses (3) Mules 23 Div	
"	10		Admitted (1) Mare 23 Div Evacuated (9) Horses (1) Mule to Base Vet Hosp. Evacuated (8) Horses (2) Mule L.S.B.C.	
"	11		Admitted (2) Horses 23 Div	
"	12		Admitted (2) Horses 23 Div Evacuated (7) Horses to Base Vety Hospital	
Barlin	13		Admitted (3) Horses (1) Army Signals (1) 170 Hy Bty (1) 35 Bty R.F.A.	
"	14		Admitted (1) Horses (1) Mule (1) 21 Div (1) 17 Bty R.F.A.	
"	15		Admitted (3) Horses (5) Horses (1) Mule sent to D.A.C. 23 Div	
"	16		Admitted (5) Mares 23 Div Evacuated (1) Mule to Base Vety Hospl (5) Horses (1) Mule to D.A. Coll

WAR DIARY
or
INTELLIGENCE SUMMARY
(Erase heading not required.)

Army Form C. 2118.

Place	Date	Hour	Summary of Events and Information	Remarks and references to Appendices
BARLIN	17.5.16	—	Admitted (2) Horses (1) Mule (9) 23 Div. (1) 2 & 6 Bays R.F.A. 0.1.5 "Bebel Club" B/112 Ay. Bty. R.F.A	
"	18			
"	19		Admitted (3) Horses (1) Mule (3) 23 Div. (1) 71 "B" A.R.F.A. Evacuated (1) B/Horses (3) Mules to Base Vet. Hospital	
"	20		Admitted (5) Horses (3) Mules 23 Div	
"	21		Admitted (3) Horses (1) 23 Div. (2) 70 "B" Bty. R.F.A. Evacuated (10) Horses (2) Mules to Base Vet. Hospital (1) Horse Revevered	
"	22		Admitted (1) Horses (1) Mule (9) 23 Div. (2) 5" Bty. R.F.E. 2 Div.	
"	23		Admitted (5) Horses Evacuated (8) Horses to Base Vet. Hosp.(1) Horse Discharged. Another Admission	
"	24		Admitted (5) Horses (1) Mule 23 Div.	
"	25		Admitted (3) Horses (2) 23 Div. (1) 2.C/B/A.R.F.A.	
"	26		Admitted (5) Horses (3) "A" Sup. 114 Bty. (5) 23 Div. (1) Destroyed Skull Inj.	
"	27		Admitted (5) Horses (4) Mules 23 Div. Evacuated (1) Horses (3) Mules to Base Vet. Hosp.	
"	28		Admitted (1) Horse (1) Mule 23 Div.	
"	29		Admitted (1) Horse 110 Hy. Bty. R.F.A	
"	30		Admitted (2) Horses (2) 23 Div. (1) 110 Hy. B. R.E. 4 5 Div.	
"	31		Admitted (3) Horses (1) Mule 23 Div.	

R.V. Ellinson
Capt. A.V.C.

35th MOBILE VETERINARY SECTION — A.V.C.

WAR DIARY
or
INTELLIGENCE SUMMARY

(Erase heading not required.)

Army Form C. 2118.

Place	Date	Hour	Summary of Events and Information	Remarks and references to Appendices
Barlin	1.6.16		Admitted (3) Horses 2.S Div Evacuated (6) Horses (3) Mules to 13 aux Vety Hospl	
"	2.6.16		Admitted (10) Horses (1) Mule (7) 2.S Div (4) other Divisions Evacuated (10) Horses(1) Mule to B V H	
"	3.6.16		Admitted (8) Horses (3) 2.S Div (5) other Divisions Evacuated (5) Horses to B V H	
"	4.		Admitted (2) Horses (1) 2.S Div (1) 110 Hy Bty R G A	
"	5.		Admitted (6) Horses (2) 2.S Div (4) other Divisions	
"	6.		Admitted (9) Horses (2.S) Div Evacuated (2.S) Horses to B V H	
"	7.		Admitted (5) Horses (1) 2.S Div (4) other Divs	
"	8.		Admitted (4) Horses (2) 2.S Div (2) other Divs Evacuated (8) Horses to B V H	
"	9.		Admitted (1) Horse 2nd D.R.	
"	10.		Admitted (9) Horses (7) 2.S Div (2) other Divs	
"	11.		Admitted (10) Horses (4) Mules 2.S Div Evacuated (13) Horses (3) Mules	
"	12.		Admitted (1) Horse 2.S Div	
"	13.		Admitted (16) Horses Destroyed (2) Evacuated (20) Horses (3) Mules	
"	14.		Marched over (1) Horse to 3rd Aux M.V.S.	
"	15.		—	
Bruay	16.		Marched to BOMY	
Bomy	17.			
"	18.		Admitted (1) Horse 2.S Div	
"	19.		Admitted (1) Horse 2.S Div	
"	20.		Admitted (20) Horses 2.S Div Evacuated (18) Horses to B V H	
"	21.			
"	22.		Admitted (1) Horse 2.S Div	

R L Allman
Capt A V C

Army Form C. 2118.

WAR DIARY
or
INTELLIGENCE SUMMARY
(Erase heading not required.)

Instructions regarding War Diaries and Intelligence Summaries are contained in F. S. Regs., Part II. and the Staff Manual respectively. Title Pages will be prepared in manuscript.

Place	Date	Hour	Summary of Events and Information	Remarks and references to Appendices
Bory	23.6.16		Admitted (7) Horses (3) Mules (2.3) Own Evacuated (14) Horses (3) Mules to B.V.H.	
	24.6.16		Marched to R.D.11.79	
	25		Entrenched	
March	26		Admitted (1) Horse (1) Destroyed Lymphangitis	
"	27		Admitted (7) Horses 2s Own	
"	28		Admitted (3) Horses (3) Mules 2s Own	
"	29		Admitted (9) Horses 2s Own Evacuated (7) Horses (3) Mules to B.V.H.	
"	30		Admitted (4) Horses 2s Own (2) Returned Evacuated (10) Horses to B.V.H.	

R.I.Milne
Capt. A.V.C.

[Stamp: 35th MOBILE VETERINARY SECTION A.V.C.]

Army Form C. 2118.

WAR DIARY
or
INTELLIGENCE SUMMARY
(Erase heading not required.)

Instructions regarding War Diaries and Intelligence Summaries are contained in F. S. Regs., Part II. and the Staff Manual respectively. Title Pages will be prepared in manuscript.

[Stamp: 36th MOBILE VETERINARY SEC · A.V.C.]

R.P. Allman Capt A.V.C.

Place	Date	Hour	Summary of Events and Information	Remarks and references to Appendices
St Frahn	1/7/16		Admitted (2) Horses 2 S Dis	
"	2		-	
"	3		Admitted (6) Horses 2 S Dis	
"	4		Admitted (2) Horses (3) Mules (1) 2S Dis (2) other Dis Evacuated (10) Horses to B.V.H.	
"	5		Admitted (8) Horses (7) 2 S Dis (1) other Dis	
"	6		Admitted (4) Horses Evacuated (8) Horses (1) Mule to B.V.H.	
Ridgement	7		Admitted (4) Horses (2) 2 S Dis (2) other Dis Destroyed (2) Horses	
"	8		Admitted (4) Horses (1) Mule (3) 2 S Dis (2) other Dis	
"	9		Admitted (3) Horses (1) Mule 2S Dis Evacuated (10) Horses (1) Mule to B.V.H.	
"	10		Admitted (4) Horses (2 S) Dis (1) Poisoned	
"	11		Admitted (4) Horses (3) 2S Dis (1) other Dis	
"	12		Admitted (12) Horses (5) 2S Dis (7) other Dis	
"	13		Admitted (7) Horses (2) Mules (6/25 Dis) (3) other Dis Evacuated (19) Horses (2) Mules to B.V.H.	
"	14		Admitted (30) Horses (2) Mules (18/2S Dis) (10) other Dis	
"	15		Admitted (7) Horses (4) 2S Dis (3) other Dis Evacuated (18) Horses (3) Mules to B.V.H.	
"	16		Admitted (8) Horses (1) Destroyed (6) 2S Dis (3) other Dis	
"	17		Admitted (4) Horses (5) Mules (2) 2 S Dis (7) other Dis	
"	18		-	
"	19		Admitted (1) Horse (1) Donkey ed 2S Dis Evacuated (14) Horses (1) Mule to B.V.H.	
"	20		Admitted (7) Horses (3) Mules (9)2S Dis (1) other Dis	
"	21		Admitted (7) Horses other Dis Evacuated (9) Horses (3) Mules to B.V.H.	
"	22		Admitted (9) Horses (2) Mules 2S Dis	
"	23		Admitted (4) Horses 2SDis Evacuated (10) Horses (2) Mules to B.V.H.	

Army Form C. 2118.

WAR DIARY
or
INTELLIGENCE SUMMARY
(Erase heading not required.)

Instructions regarding War Diaries and Intelligence Summaries are contained in F. S. Regs., Part II. and the Staff Manual respectively. Title Pages will be prepared in manuscript.

Place	Date	Hour	Summary of Events and Information	Remarks and references to Appendices
Piedmont	24.1.1.		Admitted (10) Horses (1) Mule (5) 2.3 Divl (6) other Divs (1) Returned	
"	25		Admitted (7) Horses (1) Mule (5) 2.3 Divl (6) other Divs. Evacuated (16) Horses (1) Mule to 13. V.H.	
"	26		Admitted (5) Horses (1) Mule (3) 2.3 Divl (3) other Divs	
"	27		Admitted (6) Mules (2) Mules 2.3 Divl. Evacuated (12) Horses (2) Mules to 13. V.H.	
"	28		Admitted (3) Horses (1) Mule 2.3 D-l	
"	29		Admitted (1) Mule 2.3 Divl Evacuated (9) Horses (3) Mules to 13. V.H.	
"	30		Remained (2) Horses	
"	31		Admitted (1) Horse (1) Mule	

R.L. Robinson
Capt. A.V.C.

35th MOBILE VETERINARY A.V.C.

WAR DIARY
or
INTELLIGENCE SUMMARY

(Erase heading not required.)

Army Form C. 2118.

O.C. 35 Mobile Veterinary Section   August 1918.   Vol 16

Place	Date	Hour	Summary of Events and Information	Remarks and references to Appendices
Hebuterne	1/8		Admitted 9 sick horses	
"	2 "		Admitted 8 sick horses, 2 sick mules	
"	3 "		Admitted 12 sick horses, 1 sick mule	
"	4 "		Admitted 5 sick horses, evacuated to Three Veterinary Hospital 43 sick horses, 4 sick mules	
"	5 "		Admitted 2 sick horses	
"	6 "		Admitted 6 sick horses and 1 mule	
"	7 "		Admitted 9 sick horses	
"	8 "		Admitted 10 sick horses and 1 mule	
"	9 "		Admitted 8 sick horses	
"	10 "		Admitted 5 sick horses, evacuated to Three Veterinary Hospital 38 sick horses, 2 sick mules	
"	11 "		Admitted 14 sick horses	
"	12 "		Admitted 7 sick horses and 2 mules	
"	13 "		Admitted 3 sick horses	
"	14 "		Evacuated 26 sick horses and 2 mules, struck camp and marched to Fonquevillers	
Fonquevillers	16 "		Marched to Souervon	
Souervon	17 "		Marched to Vaillent and entrained	
Fonquevillers	18 "		Arrived at Godewaersvelde, motored lorries and marched to Mont-des-Cats	
Mont-des-Cats	19 "		Marched to Pont-hieppe and took over camp with 20 sick horses from 33 Mobile Vety Section	
"	20 "		Admitted 29 sick horses	
"	21 "		Admitted 14 sick horses, evacuated to Three Veterinary Hospital 63 sick horses	

Army Form C. 2118.

WAR DIARY
or
INTELLIGENCE SUMMARY
(Erase heading not required.)

Instructions regarding War Diaries and Intelligence Summaries are contained in F. S. Regs., Part II. and the Staff Manual respectively. Title Pages will be prepared in manuscript.

Place	Date	Hour	Summary of Events and Information	Remarks and references to Appendices
Suttilffe	22/7/6		Admitted 12 sick horses.	
"	23 "		Admitted 5 sick horses and 1 mule	
"	24 "		Admitted 7 sick horses	
"	25 "		Admitted 9 sick horses and 2 mules. Evacuated 10 sick horses by Barge	
"	26 "		Admitted 8 sick horses	
"	27 "		Admitted 4 sick horses	
"	28 "		Admitted 4 sick horses. Evacuated 40 sick horses and 3 mules	
"	29 "		Admitted 4 sick horses	
"	30 "		Admitted 5 sick horses and 1 mule	
"	31 "		Admitted 8 sick horses.	

J. J. Hilliard
Capt. A.V.C.
for O.C.
33 Mobile Veterinary Section

O.C.
33 Mobile Vety Section

WAR DIARY or **INTELLIGENCE SUMMARY**
(Erase heading not required.)

Army Form C. 2118.

September 1916. Vol. 11

Place	Date	Hour	Summary of Events and Information	Remarks and references to Appendices
Dieppe	Sep 1		7 sick horses admitted	
"	2		10 sick horses, 1 sick mule admitted	
"	3		4 sick horses, 3 sick mules admitted, 19 sick horses, 2 sick mules evacuated to Base Veterinary Hospital	
"	4		46 sick horses, 1 sick mule admitted	
"	5		6 sick horses admitted, 4 sick horses, 3 sick mules evacuated to Base Vety Hospital	
"	6		51 sick horses, 1 sick mule evacuated. 4 sick horses transferred to 31st Mobile Vety Section, 35 Mobile Vety Section marched to Hazebrouck	
Hazebrouck	7		35 Mobile Vety Section marched to Ilques	
Ilques	8		1 sick horse admitted	
"	9		1 sick horse, 2 sick mules admitted, 1 sick horse, 2 sick mules evacuated to Base Vety Hospital	
"	10		Entrained at Arques	
"	11		Detrained at Saleux, marched to Allonville	
Allonville	12		1 sick horse admitted	
"	13		Section marched to St Gratien. 10 sick horses, 1 sick mule admitted	
St Gratien	14		7 sick horses admitted	

Army Form C. 2118.

WAR DIARY
or
INTELLIGENCE SUMMARY
(Erase heading not required.)

Instructions regarding War Diaries and Intelligence Summaries are contained in F. S. Regs., Part II. and the Staff Manual respectively. Title Pages will be prepared in manuscript.

Place	Date	Hour	Summary of Events and Information	Remarks and references to Appendices
St Eloien	15 Sep		5 sick horses admitted, 1 sick horse, 1 sick mule evacuated to Base Vety Hospital	
	16		2 sick horses, 1 sick mule admitted	
	17		5 sick horses admitted	
	19		17 sick horses, 1 sick mule evacuated to Base Vety Hospital	
	20		35 Mobile Vety Section marched to Albert, 5 sick horses taken over from 29th Mobile Vety Section, 1 sick horse admitted	
Albert	21		2 sick horses admitted, 4 sick horses evacuated to Base Vety Hospital	
"	23		5 sick horses, 1 sick mule admitted, 3 sick horses evacuated to 46 Mobile Vety Section (Collecting Station)	
"	24		3 sick horses, 1 sick mule admitted	
"	25		4 sick horses, 1 sick mule admitted, 12 sick horses, 3 sick mules evacuated to 46 Mobile Vety Section (Collecting Station)	
"	26		13 sick horses, 1 sick mule admitted, 4 sick horses evacuated to 46 Mobile Vety Section (Collecting Station)	
"	27		5 sick horses admitted, 9 sick horses, 1 sick mule evacuated to 46 Mobile Vety Section (Collecting Station)	
"	28		6 sick horses admitted, 6 sick horses evacuated to 46 Mobile Vety Section (Collecting Station)	
"	29		2 sick horses, 1 sick mule admitted	
"	30		3 sick horses, 1 sick mule admitted, 1 sick horse evacuated to Base Vety Hospital	

R.C. Allman Capt A.V.C.
O.C. 35 Mobile Vety Section

Army Form C. 2118.

O.C. 35 Mobile Veterinary Section

WAR DIARY
or
INTELLIGENCE SUMMARY
(Erase heading not required.)

Instructions regarding War Diaries and Intelligence Summaries are contained in F. S. Regs., Part II. and the Staff Manual respectively. Title Pages will be prepared in manuscript.

Place	Date	Hour	Summary of Events and Information	Remarks and references to Appendices
Albert	1/10/16		Admitted 9 Horses and 1 mule. Evacuated 12 Horses and 3 mules	
"	2/10/16		Admitted 1 horse	
"	3/10/16		Admitted 15 Horses and 3 mules	
"	4/10/16		Evacuated to Base Vety. Hospital 4 Horses and 1 mule	
"	5/10/16		Admitted 8 Horses and 2 mules	
"	6-10-16		Admitted 12 Horses and 1 mule. 1 Horse with abrasined wounds destroyed	
"	7-10-16		Admitted 16 Horses	
"	8-10-16		Admitted 4 Horses and 2 mules. Evacuated to Base Vety. Hospital 4 Horses 5 mules	
"	9-10-16		Admitted 15 Horses and 3 mules. Evacuated to 11th Northumbrian Fields Vety Co 5 12 16 Horses and 3 mules. Marched to N. Gralien.	
N. Gralien	11-10-16		Admitted 3 mules	
"	13-10-16		Admitted 3.4 Horses	
"	14-10-16		Admitted 2 Horses and 1 mule. Evacuated to Base Vety. Hospital 34 Horses and 3 mules	
"	15-10-16		Admitted 3 Horses and 1 mule	
"	17-10-16		Admitted 2 Horses	
"	18-10-16		Admitted 11 Horses. Shifted Camp to another site in Village	
"	19-10-16		Admitted 3 Horses	
"	20-10-16		Admitted 2 Horses and 1 mule. Evacuated to Base Vety. Hospital 22 Horses and 2 mules	

O.C. 35 Mobile Veterinary Section

WAR DIARY
or
INTELLIGENCE SUMMARY

(Erase heading not required.)

October

Army Form C. 2118.

Place	Date	Hour	Summary of Events and Information	Remarks and references to Appendices
At Eratum	21-10-16		Admitted 13 Horses	
"	22-10-16		Admitted 5 Horses	
"	23-10-16		Admitted 3 Horses. Collected 1 Horse. Evacuated to Base Vety Hospital 20 Horses and 1 Mule	
"	24-10-16		Admitted 3 Horses. Collected 1 Horse	
"	25-10-16		Admitted 8 Horses. Collected 3 Horses	
"	26-10-16		Admitted 1 Horse. Collected 1 Horse. Evacuated to Base Vety Hospital 18 Horses	
"	27-10-16		Admitted 30 Horses	
"	28-10-16		Admitted 19 Horses	
"	29-10-16		Admitted 23 Horses and 1 Mule. Evacuated to Base Vety Hospital 50 Horses	
"	30-10-16		Admitted 39 Horses. Collected 1 Horse	
"	31-10-16		Admitted 11 Horses. Evacuated to Base Vety Hospital 68 Horses and 1 Mule	

K.L. Wilson
Capt. A.V.C.
O.C. 35 Mobile Vety Section

Army Form C. 2118.

WAR DIARY
or
INTELLIGENCE SUMMARY

(Erase heading not required.)

O.C. 35th Mobile Veterinary Section   November, 1916.

Place	Date	Hour	Summary of Events and Information	Remarks and references to Appendices
Mr Erabim	1-11-16		Admitted 2 Horses, collected 1 Horse from Inhabitant (left by 1st Anzac Mtd troops)	
"	2-11-16		Admitted 6 Horses, 3 Mules	
"	3-11-16		Admitted 2 Horses	
"	4-11-16		Admitted 1 Horse, collected 1 Horse from Inhabitant (left by 237 Bty R.F.A.)	
"	5-11-16		Admitted 10 Horses, evacuated to Base Vety Hospital 25 Horses, 3 Mules	
"	6-11-16		Admitted 2 Horses	
"	7-11-16		Admitted 8 Horses	
"	8-11-16		Admitted 10 Horses	
"	9-11-16		Admitted 8 Horses, evacuated to Base Vety Hospital 24 Horses, collected 1 Horse from Inhabitant (left by 12th Royal Scots)	
"	10-11-16		Admitted 8 Horses	
"	11-11-16		Admitted 13 Horses, 3 Mules, evacuated to Base Vety Hospital 24 Horses	
"	12-11-16		Admitted 29 Horses, 1 Mule, collected 1 Horse from Inhabitant (left by 6th Seaforth Highlanders)	
"	13-11-16		Admitted 26 Horses, evacuated to Base Vety Hospital 36 Horses, 4 Mules	
"	14-11-16		Admitted 6 Horses, transferred 1 Horse to 4th Army Field Remount Section	
"	15-11-16		Admitted 8 Horses, 1 Mule	
"	16-11-16		Admitted 1 Horse	
"	17-11-16		Admitted 11 Horses, evacuated to Base Vety Hospital 14 Horses, 1 Mule	
"	18-11-16		Admitted 6 Horses, 1 Horse with Debility died, 2 Horses with Debility destroyed	
"	19-11-16		Admitted 2 Horses	
"	20-11-16		Admitted 10 Horses, 1 Mule, 3 Horses with Debility destroyed	

Army Form C. 2118.

WAR DIARY
or
INTELLIGENCE SUMMARY

(Erase heading not required.)

Instructions regarding War Diaries and Intelligence Summaries are contained in F. S. Regs., Part II. and the Staff Manual respectively. Title Pages will be prepared in manuscript.

35th MOBILE VETERINARY SECTION
Date 3-12-16
A.V.C.

Place	Date	Hour	Summary of Events and Information	Remarks and references to Appendices
Meaulte	21-11-16		Admitted 16 Horses, evacuated to Base Vety Hospital 38 Horses, 1 Mule	
"	22-11-16		Admitted 3 Horses, 2 Mules	
"	23-11-16		Collected 2 Horses from Inhabitants (left by 28th Coy Divn: A.S.C.)	
"	24-11-16		Admitted 1 Horse	
"	25-11-16		Admitted 11 Horses	
"	26-11-16		Admitted 5 Horses, evacuated to Base Vety Hospital 18 Horses, 3 Mules.	
"	27-11-16		Admitted 6 Horses	

R.C. Allanson Capt. A.V.C.
O.C. 35 Mobile Vety Section

War Diary   November. 1916.
    from
O.C. 35 Mobile Veterinary Section

Army Form C. 2118.

O.C. 35 Mobile Vety Section

WAR DIARY
or
INTELLIGENCE SUMMARY

December, 1916.

VOL / 4

(Erase heading not required.)

Instructions regarding War Diaries and Intelligence Summaries are contained in F. S. Regs., Part II. and the Staff Manual respectively. Title Pages will be prepared in manuscript.

Place	Date	Hour	Summary of Events and Information	Remarks and references to Appendices
St Gratien	1-12-16		1 Sick Horse admitted	
"	2-12-16		3 Sick Horses collected from Inhabitants. 2 Horses re-issued to 4th Army Sub Remount Section	
"	4-12-16		1 Sick Horse admitted	
"	5-12-16		1 Sick Horse admitted. 14 Horses evacuated to Base Veterinary Hospital	
Villers Bocage	7-12-16		Marched to Villers Bocage, Somme	
Rainy	8-12-16		Marched to Rainy, Somme	
Monchel	10-12-16		Marched to Monchel, Pas de Calais	
Sirieme	12-12-16		Marched to Sirieme, St Pol	
Lignyles Aire	13-12-16		Marched to Ligny les Aire, Pas de Calais	
Thiennes	14-12-16		Marched to Thiennes, Nord	
Ruyveld	16-12-16		Marched to Ruyveld, took billet No 3 Sick Horse Hoff	
Steenvoorde	18-12-16		Marched to Steenvoorde, Nord	
"	22-12-16		Admitted 1 sick horse, 1 sick mule	
"	23-12-16		Admitted 4 sick horses, 1 sick mule. Evacuated to Base Vety Hospital 1+6 Sick Horses 2 sick mules	
"	25-12-16		Admitted 9 sick Horses	
"	26-12-16		Admitted 4+1 sick horses, 1 sick mule. Evacuated to Base Vety Hospital 50 sick horses, 1 sick mule	

Army Form C. 2118.

WAR DIARY
or
INTELLIGENCE SUMMARY
(Erase heading not required.)

Instructions regarding War Diaries and Intelligence Summaries are contained in F. S. Regs., Part II. and the Staff Manual respectively. Title Pages will be prepared in manuscript.

Place	Date	Hour	Summary of Events and Information	Remarks and references to Appendices
Skumborde	27-12-16		Marched to Spheringhe	
Spheringhe	28-12-16		Admitted 2 sick horses	
	29-12-16		Admitted 1 sick horse	
	31-12-16		Evacuated 1 convalescent horse to H.Q. No. 23rd D.A.C.	

R.C. Ashman Capt- A.V.C.
O.C. 35 Mobile Vety Section

Vol 15   War Diary   January 1917.

O.C.

35 Mobile Veterinary Section

Army Form C. 2118.

O.C. Mobile Veterinary Section
33rd Mobile Veterinary Section   January, 1917.

WAR DIARY
or
INTELLIGENCE SUMMARY

(Erase heading not required.)

Instructions regarding War Diaries and Intelligence Summaries are contained in F. S. Regs., Part II. and the Staff Manual respectively. Title Pages will be prepared in manuscript.

Place	Date	Hour	Summary of Events and Information	Remarks and references to Appendices
Beninghen	1/1/17		Admitted 10 Horses and 1 Mule	
"	2/1/17		Admitted 16 Horses and 1 Mule	
"	3/1/17		Admitted 3 Horses and 3 Mules, Evacuated to Base Vety Hospital 29 Horses 2 Mules	
"	4/1/17		Admitted 3 Horses and 1 Mule	
"	5/1/17		Admitted 4 Horses and 1 Mule	
"	6/1/17		Admitted 4 Horses, Evacuated to Base Vety Hospital 14 Horses and 5 Mules	
"	9/1/17		Admitted 1 Horse and 1 Mule	
"	10/1/17		Admitted 4 Horses and 1 Mule	
"	11/1/17		Admitted 4 Horses and 3 Mules	
"	12/1/17		Admitted 13 Horses and 3 Mules	
"	13/1/17		Admitted 6 Horses, Evacuated to Base Vety Hospital 30 Horses and 8 Mules	
"	14/1/17		Admitted 2 Horses	
"	15/1/17		Admitted 6 Horses	
"	16/1/17		Admitted 1 Horse	
"	18/1/17		Admitted 54 Horses	
"	19/1/17		Admitted 4 Horses and 2 Mules, Evacuated to Base Vety Hospital 54 Horses	
"	20/1/17		Evacuated to Base Veterinary Hospital 22 Horses and 2 Mules	
"	22/1/17		Admitted 1 Horse	

Army Form C. 2118.

WAR DIARY
or
INTELLIGENCE SUMMARY

(Erase heading not required.)

Instructions regarding War Diaries and Intelligence Summaries are contained in F. S. Regs., Part II and the Staff Manual respectively. Title Pages will be prepared in manuscript.

Place	Date	Hour	Summary of Events and Information	Remarks and references to Appendices
Beerburgh	24/7/		Admitted 2 Horses	
"	25/7/		Admitted 9 Horses	
"	26/7/		Admitted 29 Horses and 2 Mules	
"	27/7/		Evacuated to Base Veterinary Hospital 34 Horses and 1 Mule. Destroyed 3 Horses with Mange and Debility	
"	28/7/		Admitted 1 Horse.	

R.C. Wilmer Capt. A.V.C.
O.C. 33 Mobile Veterinary Section.

Sp 16

February 1917

War Diary

O C 35 Mobile Veterinary Section

Army Form C. 2118.

O.C. 35 Mobile Veterinary Section   **WAR DIARY** *or* **INTELLIGENCE SUMMARY**   February. 1917.

(Erase heading not required.)

Instructions regarding War Diaries and Intelligence Summaries are contained in F. S. Regs., Part II. and the Staff Manual respectively. Title Pages will be prepared in manuscript.

Place	Date	Hour	Summary of Events and Information	Remarks and references to Appendices
Sphinxoghe	1-2-17		Admitted 2 sick horses. Building stall	
	2-2-17		Admitted 2 sick horses. Building stall	
"	3/2/17		Fatigue party building stall for sick horses in camp	
"	8-2-17		Admitted 2 sick horses. Building stall	
"	9-2-17		Admitted 3 surplus mules. Building stall	
"	10-2-17		Building stall	
"	11/Feb/17		Building stall evacuated 54 mange cases from Veterinary	
"	14-2-17		Admitted 2 sick horses	
"	15/Feb/17		Building stall. evacuated 3 sick horses	
"	19-2-17		Admitted 2 sick horses. Received 1 horse and 4 mules	
"	20-2-17		Building stall	
"	21-2-17		Admitted 3 surplus horses	
"	22-2-17		Admitted 1 sick horse	
"	23-2-17		Admitted 5 sick horses and 2 horses + 1 mule surplus received 4 horses and 2 mules	
"	24/2/17		Admitted 21 sick horses, evacuated 48 sick horses most mange	
"	25/2/17		Admitted 3 sick horses and 3 sick mules	
"	26/2/17		Admitted 1 sick horse and 2 sick mules	
"	27/2/17		Admitted 6 sick horses, evacuated 1 sick horse and 1 sick mule	
"	28/2/17		Admitted 5 sick horses.	

J.J. Hillary
for O.C. M.V. Sect.

2449 Wt. W14957/Mgo 750,000 1/16 J.B.C. & A. Forms/C.2118/12.

O.C.
35 Mobile Veterinary Section WAR DIARY
or
INTELLIGENCE SUMMARY
(Erase heading not required.)

March, 1917.

Army Form C. 2118.

Vol 17

Place	Date	Hour	Summary of Events and Information	Remarks and references to Appendices
Poperinghe	1/3/17		Transferred 15 sick horses 4 sick mules to 50th Mobile Vety Section & marched to HERZEELE	
Herzeele	2/3/17		Marched to ZEGGAR CAPPEL	
Zeggar Cappel	3/3/17		Marched to HOULLE	
Houlle	4/3/17		Preparing horse lines and camps	
"	5/3/17		Admitted 25 sick horses, evacuated 25 sick horses to Base Vety Hospital	
"	6 —		Admitted 34 sick horses and 1 sick mule, evacuated 32 sick horses and 1 sick mule to B.V.H.	
"	7 —		Admitted 2 sick horses, evacuated 4 sick horses to Base Vety Hospital.	
"	9 —		Admitted 12 sick horses	
"	10 —		Admitted 2 sick horses, evacuated 11 sick horses to Base Vety Hospital.	
"	12 —		Admitted 2 sick horses	
"	13 —		Admitted 3 sick horses and 1 sick mule.	
"	14 —		Admitted 29 sick horses, evacuated 33 sick horses and 1 sick mule to Base Vety Hospital	
"	15 —		Admitted 1 sick horse and 1 sick mule.	
"	16 —		Admitted 3 sick horses. Received 3 H.Q. Horses to Unit: cured.	
"	17 —		Admitted 20 sick horses. Evacuated 24 sick horses and 1 sick mule to Base Vety Hospital	
"	18 —		Admitted 10 sick horses and 4 sick mules, Evacuated 11 sick horses and 3 sick mules to B.V.H.	
"	19 —		Admitted 10 sick horses and 1 sick mule, Evacuated 9 sick horses and 1 sick mule to Base Vety Hospital	
"	20 —		Evacuated 1 sick horse and 1 sick mule to Base Vety Hospital, Marched to LEDERZEELE.	
Herzeele	21 —		Marched to HERZEELE.	

Army Form C. 2118.

WAR DIARY
or
INTELLIGENCE SUMMARY
(Erase heading not required.)

Instructions regarding War Diaries and Intelligence Summaries are contained in F. S. Regs., Part II. and the Staff Manual respectively. Title Pages will be prepared in manuscript.

Place	Date	Hour	Summary of Events and Information	Remarks and references to Appendices
Mazule	23/3		Collected 1 sick horse left with Subdivision	
"	24		Collected 1 — D° — D° —	
"	25		Admitted 23 sick horses	
"	26		Admitted 7 sick horses and 4 sick mules. Evacuated 26 sick horses and 4 sick mules to 19 V.H.	
"	27		Admitted 1 sick horse and 1 sick mule	
"	30		Admitted 4 sick horses	
"	31		Admitted 1 sick horse and 2 sick mules. Evacuated to 193 C. A.d.C. 1 HD horse cases	

R P Allmer
Capt. A.V.C.
O.C. 35 Mobile Vety Section.

Army Form C. 2118.

WAR DIARY
or
INTELLIGENCE SUMMARY
(Erase heading not required.)

O.C. 35 Mobile Veterinary Section

April, 1919.

Vol / 8

Instructions regarding War Diaries and Intelligence Summaries are contained in F.S. Regs., Part II. and the Staff Manual respectively. Title Pages will be prepared in manuscript.

Place	Date	Hour	Summary of Events and Information	Remarks and references to Appendices
Mingole	1/4/19		Admitted 24 sick horses	
"	2 —		Admitted 22 sick horses, 3 sick mules. Evacuated to Base Vety Hospital 28 Horses and 2 mules	
"	3 —		Admitted 3 sick horses	
"	4 —		Admitted 1 sick horse. Received 1 mule, cured.	
"	5 —		Admitted 3 sick horses. Evacuated to Base Vety Hospital 1 Horse and 1 mule.	
"	7 —		Admitted 3 sick horses. Evacuated to B.V.H. 1 horse and 1 mule. 1 horse died Debility	
"	8 —		Admitted 1 sick horse	
"	9 —		Admitted 1 sick mule. Evacuated to B.V.H. 15 horses and 1 mule	
"	10 —		Struck camp and marched to Sopenagha. Admitted 3 sick horses and took over from B.V.H. Mobile Veterinary Section 13 sick horses. Received 1 mule cured. 1 horse died Debility and Mange	
Sopinagha	12/4/19		Admitted 2 sick horses	
"	13 —		Admitted 2 sick horses, evacuated to B.V.H. 10 horses and 2 mules	
"	14 —		Admitted 1 sick horse, 2 sick mules	
"	15 —		Admitted 3 sick horses, 1 sick mule	
"	16 —		Admitted 3 sick horses	
"	17 —		Admitted 1 sick horse	
"	18 —		Admitted 3 sick horses	
"	19 —		Admitted 1 sick mule. Received 1 horse cured.	
"	20 —		Admitted 1 sick horse, 2 sick mules, evacuated to B.V.H. 4 horses and 6 mules	
"	22 —		Received 1 horse cured.	
"	23 —		Admitted 1 sick horse	
"	24 —		Admitted 2 sick horses	

Army Form C. 2118.

WAR DIARY
or
INTELLIGENCE SUMMARY
(Erase heading not required.)

O.C. 35 Mobile Veterinary Section   April 1917.

Instructions regarding War Diaries and Intelligence Summaries are contained in F.S. Regs., Part II. and the Staff Manual respectively. Title Pages will be prepared in manuscript.

Place	Date	Hour	Summary of Events and Information	Remarks and references to Appendices
Épinoy	26/4		Admitted 12 sick horses & evac. photo	
"	27		Admitted 1 sick horse. 1 sick mule evacuated to 13 V.H. 12 horses and 4 mules	
"	30		Admitted 2 sick horses, 1 sick mule.	

R C Allman
Capt. A.V.C.
O.C. 35 Mobile Veterinary Section

Army Form C. 2118.

WAR DIARY
or
INTELLIGENCE SUMMARY
(Erase heading not required.)

O.C. 35th Mobile Veterinary Section
May 1917
Vol 19

Place	Date	Hour	Summary of Events and Information	Remarks and references to Appendices
Shorapur	1/5		Admitted 3 sick horses and 2 sick mules	
"	2/5		Handed over 8 sick horses and 5 sick mules with camp to O.C. 31 Mobile Vety Section. Marched to Koyeld.	
Koyeld	4/5		Admitted 2 sick mules	
"	5/5		Admitted 4 sick horses	
"	6		Admitted 2 sick horses, received 1 sick mule	
"	7		Admitted 1 sick horse and 3 sick mules. Evacuated to Base Vety Hospital 4 horses and 2 mules	
"	8		Admitted 4 sick horses	
"	9		Admitted 3 sick horses	
"	10		Admitted 5 sick horses and 4 sick mules	
"	12		Admitted 22 sick horses and 4 sick mules	
"			Evacuated to Base Vety Hospital 30 horses and 4 mules. Marched to Kurnigulur	
Kurnigulur	14		Admitted 3 sick horses	
"	15		Admitted 1 sick horse	
"	16		Admitted 6 sick horses	
"	17		Admitted 3 sick horses and 1 sick mule	
"	18		Admitted 1 sick horse. Evacuated to Base Vety Hospital 11 horses and 1 mule	
"	19		Admitted 1 sick horse	
"	20		Admitted 1 sick horse	
"	21		Admitted 15 sick horses	

O.C. 33 Mobile Veterinary Section — **WAR DIARY** or **INTELLIGENCE SUMMARY**

Army Form C. 2118.

May 1917

Place	Date	Hour	Summary of Events and Information	Remarks and references to Appendices
Remyplat	22		Admitted 1 sick horse	
"	23		Admitted 1 sick horse	
"	24		Admitted 23 sick horses and 5 sick mules	
"	25		Admitted 2 sick horses, evacuated to Base Vety Hospital 34 horses and 5 mules	
"	26		Admitted 1 sick mule. Destroyed 1 horse. Blind and Debility	
"	28		Admitted 4 sick horses	
"	29		Admitted 3 sick horses and 2 sick mules, evacuated 1 horse cured	
"	30		Admitted 2 sick horses and 2 sick mules, evacuated 1 horse cured	
"	31		Admitted 44 sick horses and 5 sick mules, evacuated 2 horses cured	

R.L. _____ AVC
O.C. 33 Mobile Veterinary Section.

Army Form C. 2118.

WAR DIARY
or
INTELLIGENCE SUMMARY
(Erase heading not required.)

35 Mobile Veterinary Section
June 1917.

VA 20

Instructions regarding War Diaries and Intelligence Summaries are contained in F. S. Regs., Part II. and the Staff Manual respectively. Title Pages will be prepared in manuscript.

Place	Date	Hour	Summary of Events and Information	Remarks and references to Appendices
Rumghest	1	—	Admitted 3 sick horses. Evacuated to Base Vety Hospital 4 sick horses, 2 sick mules	
"	2	—	Admitted 2 sick horses. Evacuated to B.V.H. 1 sick horse. Destroyed 1 mule and received record	
"	3	—	Admitted 2 sick horses	
"	4	—	Admitted 3 sick horses and 2 sick mules	
"	5	—	Admitted 3 sick horses	
"	6	—	Admitted 4+ sick horses and 7 sick mules. Evacuated to B.V.H. 2 sick horses. Received 2 horses and 1 mule cured	
"	7	—	Admitted 18 sick horses and 4 sick mules. Received 1 horse cured. Evacuated to B.V.H. 2 sick horses	
"	8	—	Admitted 3 sick horses. Evacuated to B.V.H. 55 sick horses and 10 sick mules	
"	9	—	Admitted 2 sick horses and 1 sick mule	
"	10	—	Admitted 7 sick horses and 1 sick mule. Destroyed 1 horse with Strangles around. Received 3 horses cured	
"	11	—	Admitted 4 sick horses	
"	12	—	Admitted 4 sick horses and 1 sick mule. Evacuated to X Corps Mobile Vety Detachment 23 sick horses and 3 sick mules. Received & boarded to BERTHEN	
Berthen	13	—	Admitted 11 sick horses	
"	15	—	Admitted 5 sick horses	
"	16	—	Admitted 1 sick horse. Received 3 horses cured	
"	17	—	Admitted 1 sick horse. Received 3 horses cured	
"	21	—		

Army Form C. 2118.

WAR DIARY
or
INTELLIGENCE SUMMARY

(Erase heading not required.)

Instructions regarding War Diaries and Intelligence Summaries are contained in F. S. Regs., Part II and the Staff Manual respectively. Title Pages will be prepared in manuscript.

Place	Date	Hour	Summary of Events and Information	Remarks and references to Appendices
BERTHEN	23	6/7	Admitted 8 sick horses and 2 sick mules.	
"	24		Evacuated 1 horse used.	
"	26		Admitted 2 sick horses and 1 sick mule.	
"	27		Evacuated to Base Vety Hospital 22 sick horses and 3 sick mules.	
"	28		Admitted 1 sick horse and 1 mule.	
"	29		Admitted 3 sick horses. Recovered 3 horses used.	
"	30		Admitted 1 sick horse. Evacuated to Base Vety Hospital 1 mare and foal.	

R A Ulman
Capt A.V.C.
O.C. 33rd Field Veterinary Section

O.C. 35 Mobile Veterinary Section

WAR DIARY or **INTELLIGENCE SUMMARY**
(Erase heading not required.)

July, 1917

Army Form C. 2118.

Place	Date	Hour	Summary of Events and Information	Remarks and references to Appendices
BERTHEN	1-7-17		Admitted 6 sick horses, 2 sick mules	
"	2 "		" 1 sick horse	
"	4 "		Handed over 11 sick horses and camp to 32 Mobile Veterinary Section and marched to RENINGHELST.	
RENINGHELST	4 "		Admitted 17 sick horses, 16 sick mules.	
"	5 "		" 4 sick horses	
"	6 "		" 4 sick horses, 1 sick mule, 2 horses with shell wounds died	
"	7 "		" 5 sick horses, 1 sick mule. Received 2 horses cured	
"	8 "		" 6 sick horses. Received 1 horse cured	
"	9 "		" 10 sick horses	
"	10 "		" 6 sick horses, 1 sick mule. Evacuated to Base Vety Hospital 32 horses & 13 mules	
"	11 "		" 2 sick horses, 2 sick mules, 1 mule with shell wounds destroyed	
"	12 "		" 2 sick horses, 2 sick mules	
"	13 "		" 3 sick horses, 7 sick mules. Received 1 mule cured	
"	14 "		" 15 sick horses. Received 1 horse cured.	
"	15 "		" 2 sick horses. Received 1 horse cured.	
"	16 "		" 5 sick horses. Evacuated to Base Vety Hospital 28 horses, 12 mules	
"	17 "		" 5 sick horses, 2 sick mules. Received 1 horse cured, 1 horse with catarrh died	
"	18 "		" 7 sick horses, 1 sick mule. Received 2 mules cured, 1 mule with paralysis and 2 horses with shell wounds destroyed	

Army Form C. 2118.

WAR DIARY
or
INTELLIGENCE SUMMARY
(Erase heading not required.)

Instructions regarding War Diaries and Intelligence Summaries are contained in F. S. Regs., Part II. and the Staff Manual respectively. Title Pages will be prepared in manuscript.

Place	Date	Hour	Summary of Events and Information	Remarks and references to Appendices
RENINGHELST	19-7-17		Admitted 1 sick horse, 1 horse with shell wound destroyed.	
"	20		" 9 sick horses, 3 sick mules. Evacuated 4 horses cured	
"	21		" 10 sick horses, 2 horses with shell wounds destroyed. Evacuated 4 horses and 2 mules	
"	22		" 1 sick horse. Evacuated 2 horses and 1 mule.	
"	23		Handed over 33 sick horses, 4 sick mules and camp to 36 Mobile Vety Section, Marched to BERTHEN. Admitted 2 sick horses and 2 sick mules	
BERTHEN	24		Admitted 2 sick horses. Evacuated to Base Vety Hospital 2 horses	
"	26		" 1 sick horse.	
"	27		" 1 sick horse.	
"	28		" 4 sick horses and 2 sick mules	
"	30		" 3 sick horses. Evacuated to Base Vety Hospital 8 horses and 3 mules	
"	31		" 1 sick horse	

R C Wilson Capt. A.V.C.
O.C. 35 Mobile Veterinary Section

35 Mobile Vety. Section.

WAR DIARY
INTELLIGENCE SUMMARY
(Erase heading not required.)

Army Form C. 2118.

Vol 22

Place	Date 1917 August	Hour	Summary of Events and Information	Remarks and references to Appendices
BERTHEN	1st		Admitted 1 L.D.	
"	3rd		Admitted 2 L.D. 2 Mules 1 R. Destroyed 1 L.D.	
ARQUES	5th			
Mt HULETTE	6th			
EPERLEQUES	9th		Admitted 3 L.D. 1 R., evacuated 1 R. to 23rd B.V.H.	
"	11th			
"	13th		Admitted 2 L.D. 2 R. (evacuated 5 L.D.) Died 1 L.D. to 23rd B.V.H.	
"	14th		Admitted 2 H.R. 2 R., evacuated 7 R. 2 H.D. 2 mules / to 23rd B.V.H.	
"	15th		Admitted 3 R. 1 L.D.	
"	18th		Admitted 5 R. 2 mules 1 L.D.	
"	20th		Admitted 4 H.D. 3 L.D. 2 R. evacuated 3 L.D. 1 H.D. 4 R. 1 mule to 23rd B.V.H.	
MOORPEENE	23rd			
RENINGHELST	24th		Admitted 1 2 L.D. 3 H.D. 2 R.	
"	26th		Admitted 8 L.D. 1 H.D. 4 R. evacuated 4 L.D. 3 H.D. 2 R. 1 mule to Li Bospo M.V.D.	
"	27th		Admitted 4 L.D. 7 H.D. 2 R. 3 mules.	
"	28th		Admitted 1 H.D. 2 L.D. 1 mule evacuated 8 L.D. 4 H.D. 1 mule to Li Bospo M.V.D.	
"	29th		Admitted 3 L.D. 6 mules 3 R. 1 H.D. evacuated 2 8 L.D. 4 H.D. 7 R. 1 mule to 23rd B.V.H.	
"	30th		Admitted 5 H.D. 9 L.D. 3 R. 1 mule evacuated 1 H.D. 4 L.D. 2 R. 2 mules. to Wittenhoek - AC allowance Capt A.V.C.	
"	31st		Admitted 1 H.D. 6 L.D. 3 R. 3 mules.	

OC 35 Mobile Vety Section

WAR DIARY or INTELLIGENCE SUMMARY

Army Form C. 2118.

Month Ending 5th Oct 1917

35 Mobile Veterinary Section 23rd Div

Vol 23

Place	Date	Hour	Summary of Events and Information	Remarks and references to Appendices
Lillequelt	5.9.17		Admitted 6 Horses 3 Mules. Evacuated 6 Horses 3 Mules	
	12.9.17		Admitted 4 Horses. Evacuated 4 Horses	
In La Clytte	14.9.17		Took over 8 Horses from 36 M.V.S.	
"	15.9.17		Admitted 24 Horses	
"	16.9.17		Admitted 20 Horses 1 Mule	
"	17.9.17		Admitted 11 Horses 2 Mules. Reissued 1 Horse	
"	18.9.17		Admitted 12 Horses 2 Mules. Evacuated 58 Horses, 2 Mules. Destroyed 1 Horse	
"	19.9.17		Admitted 10 Horses 2 Mules. Reissued 2 Horses	
"	22.9.17		Admitted 25 Horses 8 Mules. Evacuated 8 Horses 4 Mules. Destroyed 1 Horse	
Moved to Westoutre	25.9.17		Admitted 9 Horses 5 Mules. Evacuated up Horses 1 Mule. Handed to 23rd MVT 12 Horses 6 Mules	
Westoutre	26.9.17		Admitted 9 Horses 1 Mule. Reissued 1 Horse	
Moved to La Clytte	27.9.17		Took over 47 Horses 10 Mules from L 3rd M.V.S.	
La Clytte	28.9.17		Admitted 27 Horses 6 Mules	
"	29.9.17		Admitted 15 Horses 1 Mule. Evacuated 35 Horses 12 Mules. Destroyed 1 Horse 1 Mule Died	3rd Div
"	30.9.17		Admitted 18 Horses 10 Mules. Evacuated 1 Horse. Destroyed 1 Horse 1 Mule Died	
Moved to Berthen	2.10.17		Admitted 3 Horses. Evacuated 66 Horses 10 Mules. Handed over to 3rd MV.2. 7.10 Horses 3 Mules	
Berthen	3.10.17			
"	5.10.17		Admitted 5 Horses	

J M Hunt
for O.C. 35 Mobile Vety Section

WAR DIARY
or
INTELLIGENCE SUMMARY

(Erase heading not required.)

Army Form C. 2118.

Mob Vety Sec
No 24

Place	Date	Hour	Summary of Events and Information	Remarks and references to Appendices
Vakhtyle	1/10/17		18 Horses 11 Mules 1 Horse Evacuated.	
To Burkin	2/10/17		3 Horses 72 Horses & 13 Mules Evacuated. one man proceeded on leave	
	3/10/17		4 Horses	
	5/10/17		3 Horses. 2 Horse Evacuated.	
	6/10/17		1 Horse 3 mules 1 mule Returned to M.G.C.	
	7/10/17		1 Horse 1 mule. 1 horse Returned to 101. R.E.	
To 2nd Cav Bde	9/10/17		1 " 14 " evacuated	
	10/17		1 R reissued.	
	12/10/17		4 horses 13 Mules Admitted	
	13/10/17		9 " 1 "	
	14/10/17		7 " 1 "	
	15/10/17		12 " 1 "	
	16/10/17		11 " 2 " 30 horses 10 mules evacuated to 3 M.V.S	
	17/10/17		48 " 5 " 1 Horse 2 Mules evacuated. 1 man returning from leave	

R.C. Almon
Capt a.v.c.
OC 35th M.V.S.

Army Form C. 2118.

WAR DIARY
or
INTELLIGENCE SUMMARY

(Erase heading not required.)

Instructions regarding War Diaries and Intelligence Summaries are contained in F. S. Regs., Part II. and the Staff Manual respectively. Title Pages will be prepared in manuscript.

Place	Date	Hour	Summary of Events and Information	Remarks and references to Appendices
Ira Clyde	18/10/17		12 Horses & 3 Mules admitted. 1 Horse & 1 Mule Evacuated	
	19/10/17		5 Horses & 1 mule admitted. 4 Horses & 7 mules Evacuated to Corps M.V.S.	
	27/10/17		8 Horses & 3 mules admitted. Pte Rix reported for duty.	
	21/10/17		3 Horses & 2 mules admitted	
	22/10/17		6 Horses & 2 mules Evacuated G.23.B.V.H. To Corps	
Queenups	23/10/17		To Queenups.	
	24/10/17		3 Horses admitted.	
	26/10/17		Left Queenups & arrived at Wiganis.	
Wiganis	27/10/17		6 Horses admitted. 8 Horses Evacuated G.23 V.H.	
	28/10/17		1 Horse & 1 Mule admitted	
	29/10/17		2 Horses & 1 mule admitted. 6 Horses & 5 mules Evacuated G.23 B.V.H.	
	30/10/17		3 Horses & 2 mules admitted	
	31/10/17		2 Horses & 1 mule admitted. 4 Horses & 3 mules Evacuated G.23 V.H.	

R L Armstrong